WELCOME TO CAERLAVEROCK CASTLE

Caerlaverock Castle stands on the edge of Scotland, where the swift-flowing River Nith enters the salt marshes of the Solway Firth. For over 400 years in the Middle Ages the mighty castle guarded an important gateway into the kingdom of Scotland. Its red sandstone walls are peaceful now, but if those stones could talk they would tell of lords and lieges, wars and sieges.

The lands of Caerlaverock – the name could mean either 'fort of the skylark' or 'elm fort' – were ruled over by the British lords of Nithsdale after the Romans abandoned their hold on southern Scotland around AD 400. By about 950 the Nithsdale lords had built a fort on the site that would later become the 'old' castle. In around 1220, Alexander II of Scotland granted the lands to an incomer from the eastern Borders, Sir John de Maccuswell (Maxwell). The Maxwells built the first castle – the old castle – around 1220, but since it proved too small and prone to flooding lived in it for just 50 years. In around 1270, therefore, the Maxwells built a new castle, where they remained until 1640.

Above: This deeply carved demon's face would once have occupied a prominent position on the castle walls. Today it stares out at visitors to the tearoom!

CONTENTS

Opposite: Caerlaverock has not one castle but two, both visible in this aerial view. The older castle (top) was built in the 1220s; the newer one, 200m to the north, dates from the 1270s.

CAERLAVEROCK CASTLE AT A GLANCE

The 'new' castle at Caerlaverock is one of Scotland's great medieval fortresses. Uniquely, it is triangular in shape, with three tall towers built integrally with the curtain, or outer, wall, one at each point of the triangle. From the road above the castle, visitors can see the Solway Firth lying between Scotland and England. In the Middle Ages this proximity to England brought the castle into frequent conflict. The contemporary account of Edward I of England's siege of Caerlaverock in 1300 (see pages 26–27) is one of the most fascinating recorded for any castle in Britain.

The castle walls were rebuilt in the 1370s, after the Wars of Independence, and further alterations were made to make the fortress more suited for lordly living. The siege of 1640, however, during the Civil War between Charles I and his Scottish subjects, proved to be the castle's last, and after the Royalist garrison surrendered to the Covenanters, Caerlaverock fell into disuse.

Opposite: Caerlaverock is one of the most impressive of all Scottish castles. The uneven ground in front of the castle hides the remains of siege works, outer defences and outbuildings.

WAR AND SIEGE

26 SIEGE OF CAERLAVEROCK

In July 1300 a garrison of 60 men faced the might of Edward I's English army, an event recorded in a contemporary poem.

29 WEAPONS OF WAR

This replica trebuchet, or stone-throwing machine, reminds visitors of the many sieges the castle endured.

31 STRONG DEFENCES

Fortifications added to the castle included machicolations (slots) along the tops of the walls and, later, gun holes for artillery.

RICH STONE CARVINGS

I TERRIFYING FACES

Carved faces, such as this grotesque head, and gargoyles were used to intimidate castle visitors in the Middle Ages. Caerlaverock was no exception.

II FINE DETAILS

Decorative carvings on fireplaces and other fixtures hint at the quality of the castle's original interiors.

13 ALLEGORIES IN STONE

Carvings above the doorways and windows of the Renaissance-style Nithsdale Lodging depict allegorical scenes from classical mythology.

CASTLE LIFE

11 EVERYDAY OBJECTS

Excavations in the 1950s unearthed a rich haul of pottery vessels, leather ware and implements such as knives and combs – telling us much about everyday castle life.

21 EXOTIC GLASS

Fragments of an Islamic glass vessel, found during excavations of the old castle, make a surprising link between Caerlaverock and medieval Syria.

32 FIXTURES AND FITTINGS

An inventory of 1640 provides a fascinating glimpse into castle life shortly before Caerlaverock's abandonment.

WOODLAND TRAIL

18 COPPICING

The trees surrounding Caerlaverock were traditionally managed to ensure a yearly supply of wood.

19 FLORA

The ancient woodland habitat between the old and new castles is home to alder, oak and willow trees, as well as bluebells (right) and meadowsweet.

19 FAUNA

Inhabitants of Caerlaverock's woodland include roe deer and the endangered natterjack toad.

Nature trail →

Visitor Centre ↘

A GUIDED TOUR

This tour guides the visitor around the two castles of Caerlaverock – first the 'new', then the 'old'. Once you have completed your visit to the new castle, leave by the gatehouse, turn left immediately beyond the moat and follow the nature trail around the castle and through the woods to the old castle.

Opposite: Caerlaverock's triangular layout, planned in the late 13th century, is unique among Scottish castles.

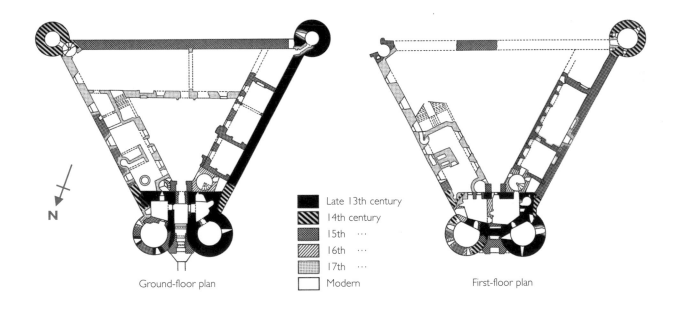

N

Ground-floor plan

Late 13th century
14th century
15th ···
16th ···
17th ···
Modern

First-floor plan

Illustration key

1 The moat and gatehouse

2 Murdoch's Tower

3 The courtyard

4 The Nithsdale Lodging

5 The nature trail

6 The old castle

'In shape it was like a shield, for it had but three sides round it, with a tower at each corner, but one of them was a double one, so high, so long and so wide, that the gate was underneath it, well made and strong, with a sufficiency of other defences . . . good walls and good ditches filled right up to the brim with water.'

(From *The Roll of Karlaverock*, composed in the summer of 1300 by a herald in Edward I of England's entourage to commemorate the successful siege of the castle.)

THE MOAT AND GATEHOUSE

T he approach to the new castle crosses uneven grassy ground showing telltale signs of past siege works, outer defensive works and castle outbuildings. Surrounding the castle are two moats, the outer one now dry but the inner one still providing a considerable expanse of water. These outer layers of defence are wrapped around a mighty courtyard castle, first laid out in the late 13th century but whose walls and towers were subsequently altered to take account of both siege damage and fashion. Even in ruins, Caerlaverock remains the epitome of the medieval stronghold.

The modern bridge over the moat replaces a drawbridge, which would have been raised by a chain passing through a square hole high above the inner arch. This drawbridge, in turn, replaced an earlier one, which worked on a horizontal axis, like a see-saw. Archaeologists excavated the moat in 1958 and discovered the remains of three phases of medieval bridge construction. Tree-ring dating subsequently showed that the first bridge was built about 1277, repaired in the 1330s and then replaced altogether by a new bridge in about 1370.

THE GATEHOUSE

The great towers flanking the gate have their origins in the 13th century. Two-thirds of the western (right-hand) tower is built of the finely jointed ashlar so typical of that time, but the eastern (left-hand) tower has few traces of early work and seems to date mostly to the 15th century. The 15th century also saw the building of the outer arch of the entrance and the chamber behind which housed the winding gear for the new portcullis. This infilling created a more unified façade and was complemented by elaborate machicolations (slotted defences for dropping missiles on enemies) at the wallhead. The 16th-century addition of the caphouse at the very top completed the front of the castle. The large stone plaque bearing the arms of the Maxwells was added above the doorway in the 17th century.

Opposite: Caerlaverock's main front, with its moat and drawbridge (now replaced by a modern bridge), was a bold expression of the power of the Maxwell lords, whose coat-of-arms (above) was added above the entrance gate in the 1600s.

THE GATEHOUSE INTERIOR AND COURTYARD

The gatehouse with its two towers fulfilled several roles. It provided an imposing entrance into the castle; the ground-floor rooms were used as guardrooms, storage cellars and a prison; and the upper storeys housed the main residential accommodation for the Maxwell family.

The entrance into the castle courtyard was along a narrow passage. This was defended first by a portcullis, the slot for which can be seen behind the first arch. Behind it was a door, the indent for which you can still see. Next was a pointed archway, which marks where the original entrance front was; above it is a fine shovel-ended arrow slit. Beyond is the original portcullis slot, disused since the outer one was added in the 15th century. There was once another door at the far end leading into the courtyard.

Below: The courtyard, with the inner arch of the gatehouse in between the west range (left) and east front of the Nithsdale Lodging (right). The structural movement visible in the stair door immediately to the left of the entrance passage is proof that the new castle was not entirely founded on solid rock.

INSIDE THE TOWERS

Within the passage doors lead off either side to guardrooms, and from them into the basements of the towers. The room on your right as you enter (the west guardroom) has a small fireplace and is largely early work except for the round-headed doorway inserted in the 15th century to give access to the basement of the tower. Prior to this entrance the ground floor was probably reached by a trapdoor from above and most likely served as a pit-prison.

At first-floor level are the remains of three original windows. The two which looked north have been blocked with later masonry – one as a result of additions to the gateway in the 15th century. At first- and second-floor levels are original doorways leading into latrine closets. All the doorways from the tower into the main part of the gatehouse above first-floor level have been replaced at some time, probably when the upper part of the tower with its fine rib-vaulted roof was added in the 15th century.

The east tower echoes the west. It is more difficult to disentangle the building history here because it has been rebuilt at least once, although traces of its early construction can be seen to the left of the door from the guardroom. The ground floor has also had a rubble stone vault inserted, as well as gun holes dating to the 16th century. Like the west tower, the upper floors would all have been made of timber, but the capping vault, while of a similar date, is much simpler.

THE COURTYARD

The courtyard was the heart of the castle, always bustling with life. When first built, the curtain walls (so-called because they were drawn around the courtyard like curtains) were lined with timber buildings. Over time the Maxwells replaced them with stone buildings, reflecting an increasing desire for comfort and display. Access to the first floor of the gatehouse was originally by a wooden stair from the courtyard on the west side of the gatehouse. This was replaced in the 15th century by a stone stair tower (the existing steps are modern), which gave access both to the gatehouse and the west range.

Above: Looking from the west guardroom to the entrance passage (top). The original timber floors are now missing from the towers, but the fine rib-vaulted ceiling in the west tower (above) survives.

THE MAXWELL LODGING

The upper floors of the gatehouse provided accommodation for the Maxwells. At first-floor level was a feasting hall. The original room is now hard to imagine as it has been much altered – you must think away the central wall and add a high stone-vaulted ceiling. The fireplace, at the east end, was larger than the present opening, which is a 17th-century replacement.

Two windows facing onto the courtyard lit the hall. The west side of the west window is intact, but its eastern jamb together with the entire eastern window has been altered. The low arch in the north wall is the blocked entrance to the 13th-century portcullis chamber.

Above top: An artist's impression of how the feasting hall in the Maxwell Lodging may have looked in about 1300. Note the portcullis chamber on the left. The same view (above) as it looks today.

At the west end of the hall a stair led to chambers on the second floor. These chambers gave access to the upper rooms in the towers on either side of the gatehouse – rooms which provided additional family living quarters.

BUILDING ALTERATIONS

This original accommodation was drastically altered by the Maxwells between the 1400s and the 1600s. In the 15th century they modified the windows, replaced the high stone vault with a lower timber ceiling and blocked the portcullis chamber. In the 16th century they put up the present cross wall to create two smaller rooms. Finally, in the 17th century, they inserted a door at the east end to give access to the new apartments in the Nithsdale Lodging (see pages 12–13).

Above: A fireplace jamb from the 17th-century alterations to the Maxwell Lodging.

EVERYDAY OBJECTS

In the 1950s and 60s, excavations in and around the moat at Caerlaverock's new castle unearthed a remarkable hoard of items, from belt buckles and leather boots to pots, pans and knives. These finds, among the best collection of medieval artefacts of domestic life discovered in Scotland, help us better understand the nature of everyday castle life.

1 Pottery jugs were commonly used to hold ale.

2 Part of a leather case that may have commemorated the marriage in 1539 of Robert, fifth Lord Maxwell, to Agnes Stewart.

3 Knives, such as these bone-handled ones, were used for many different purposes.

4 A 15th-century double-sided birchwood comb, whose heart motif suggests it was given as a love token.

The arms of Countess Beaumont
(Earl Robert's wife)

The arms of Earl Robert,
first earl of Nithsdale

A female figure reaches up to
heaven, with Human Love
beneath her

Divine Love holds scales, into
which Human Love piles the
goods of the world

THE NITHSDALE LODGING

Because they were built by Robert, first earl of Nithsdale, the ranges along the east and south sides of the courtyard are known as the Nithsdale Lodging. In 1634, the year the lodging was completed, security was no longer a priority, so Robert had large windows formed in the east curtain wall to give fine views over the moat. The public rooms in the south range were spacious and well lit, while the chambers in the east range were designed for comfort and privacy. The contrast to the medieval rooms in the gatehouse would have been stark.

The east range consists of a two-roomed apartment on each of its three floors. The rooms are awkward shapes because they had to fit around the central chimney stack serving the kitchen on the ground floor. Each room has a fireplace – the two on the first floor are the most elaborate – and most have 'en suite' toilet closets.

At the south end of the east range, a broad scale-and-platt (flight and landing) staircase leads down to the south range, which comprised a large entrance hall with a smaller room to its west. What the upper floors contained is unknown, but there must have been a fine chapel somewhere since the Maxwells were devout Catholics.

A doorway at the bottom of the grand stair leads into the ground-floor service rooms in the east range. These vaults were, in the order you pass through them: the servery; the kitchen, with its great fireplace (rebuilt in modern times to support the weight of the chimneys above); and lastly the bakehouse, with an oven in the corner of the fireplace and a well in the centre of the floor.

The façade of the Nithsdale Lodging has a feast of stone carving. Only the east range stands to its full height, but the hints of grandeur noted on the interior are confirmed in full by this magnificent exterior. When complete, it demonstrated perfect symmetry – a hallmark of Renaissance design.

Opposite: The east range of the Nithsdale Lodging – a Renaissance mansion within a medieval castle. The date stone (above) over one of the ground-floor windows records when it was built.

Below: The carved pediments on the lodging display coats-of-arms and allegorical scenes from classical mythology. Carvings 6 and 7 in particular may allude to the fortunes of the Catholic Maxwells under James VI. As punishment for their beliefs, Earl Robert's late father lay unburied for five years, and Robert himself spent years in prison.

5

Divine Love points to Human Love, who draws a figure into his boat with a net

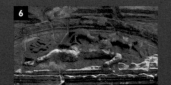

6

The corpse of Patroclus being pecked by vultures

7

Prometheus in chains having his liver pecked by an eagle

8

Neptune in a chariot, drawn by sea creatures

MURDOCH'S TOWER AND THE WEST RANGE

At either end of the south range was a round tower. The south-east tower has largely collapsed, but the south-west one, known as Murdoch's Tower, still stands to its full height. It takes its name from Murdoch, duke of Albany, a cousin of James I, who is recorded as being confined there in 1425 shortly before his execution. However, the association between Murdoch, 'the power behind the throne', and Caerlaverock seems implausible. The duke, together with his wife Isabella, his son and others in his extended family, was arrested in Perth at the end of April 1425. He was brought to trial in Stirling and executed in front of the castle there on 25 May. Why bring Murdoch all the way to Caerlaverock for his confinement when there were plenty of strong castle prisons in the Perth–Stirling area, all of which were perfectly capable of holding him?

Today, the entrance to the ground floor is a doorway, but in the past it would have been a trapdoor in the floor above, suggesting its use as a pit-prison. The first floor was accessible from a passage in the south curtain wall, and the second floor directly from the wall-walk on the west curtain wall. None of these rooms has a fireplace, and they seem therefore to have had a military function. The three small windows on the first floor have traces of narrow 13th-century arrow slits below them (best seen from outside the castle).

THE WEST RANGE

The plain front of the west range is in stark contrast to the grand façade of the Nithsdale Lodging. The two-storey block, built sometime after 1450, has three rooms on the ground floor, each entered separately from the courtyard. There would have been two further rooms on the upper level. Each room has a decorated fireplace, except the larger room on the upper floor which has two, suggesting its former use as a great hall or banqueting room. There was no internal stair linking the two floors – the upper floor was presumably reached by stairs at either end.

When you have completed your exploration of the new castle, exit by the gatehouse and follow the nature trail to the old castle. As you do so, take a moment to admire the new castle from the outside.

Above: A fish-tailed arrow slit in Murdoch's Tower, dating from the late 13th century.

Opposite: Murdoch's Tower, viewed from the east range, with part of the west range visible to the right.

Above: Decorative stonework from a fireplace in the west range.

THE CASTLE EXTERIOR

Walking around the castle gives you a sense of its strength, economy of form and pleasing geometry. With its triangular design, only three lengths of curtain wall were required, with a round tower at two of the corners and the twin-towered gatehouse at the third.

A wide moat was excavated out of the solid rock to act as a defence, and the material used to form a triangular platform on which the stone castle was built. The underlying rock actually slopes down from north to south, so that while the gatehouse is built on a solid foundation the rest of the complex is less securely founded.

THE WEST CURTAIN WALL

The west curtain wall is complete to the wallhead, but it has few features in it. The section adjoining the gatehouse was rebuilt in the 14th century and is of slightly different character from the tower. Where the two meet, projecting latrine chutes discharged into the moat. The curtain wall itself has 13th-century work on its lower levels, and a later rubble wall of simple character above, topped off with a wall-walk. There was another latrine near Murdoch's Tower. The later work is probably the rebuilding made necessary after the Wars of Independence (see pages 26–30). Murdoch's Tower also has original masonry – note the 13th-century fish-tailed arrow slits – but it too was rebuilt in the later 14th century. The machicolations (slots) at the wallhead date from the 15th century.

THE EAST CURTAIN WALL

The south curtain wall has almost entirely gone, probably intentionally demolished by the Covenanters after the 1640 siege to make the castle incapable of being held against them again (see pages 32–35). The east curtain wall, however, survives substantially intact. It has a widely splayed base, unlike the west curtain wall, which may indicate a more thorough rebuilding in the early 14th century. The large windows were inserted in the 1630s to light the Nithsdale Lodging. Like the west curtain wall, the section of wall immediately south of the gatehouse was built in the 14th century, with its wallhead machicolations added in the 15th century.

Opposite, main image:
This aerial view shows off Caerlaverock's triangular-shaped layout and its wide moat, whose waters reflect the evening shadows of Murdoch's Tower and the Nithsdale Lodging.

1   The west gatehouse tower and west curtain wall

2   The west curtain wall and Murdoch's Tower

3   The demolished south curtain wall, looking into the courtyard

4   The east curtain wall (right) and south range

THE NATURE TRAIL

The path between the new and old castles takes you through ancient woodland. Traditionally this area would have been managed for its forest products, especially oak, and as a source of shelter and fodder for cattle and deer. The storage of grass as winter food for cattle is relatively modern: prior to this people cut tree branches as fodder and allowed livestock into woodland in the autumn to feed on the seed. Many of the low banks in the wood are remnants of fences erected to prevent cattle and deer from damaging young trees.

COPPICING

Many trees surrounding the old castle show signs of having been coppiced – a way of managing woodland to provide a yearly supply of timber. Most trees when cut down will re-grow from the stump. When trimmed by hand this re-growth develops into a few strong shoots, which quickly grow into long straight poles fed by the well-developed root growth.

Above top: Bluebells carpet the nature trail between Caerlaverock's two castles in May. The trail passes through ancient woodland, a precious habitat for many plants and animals.

Above: Scotland's most important breeding colony for natterjack toads, like this one, lies in the Caerlaverock National Nature Reserve, adjacent to the castle grounds.

There are many traditional uses for coppiced wood. Coppiced willow, for example, was used for making baskets, fences, ropes, lobster pots and shafts for tools. Uses for coppiced oak included structural beams and tool handles, while oak bark was used to tan leather and oak galls (outgrowths of plant tissue) were used for ink. Coppiced oak and alder were also used for charcoal – oak charcoal in particular is good for producing the high temperature needed in ironworking, and may well have powered the smithies found around the old castle.

FLORA AND FAUNA

Lying adjacent to Caerlaverock National Nature Reserve, an area of outstanding biodiversity, the lands around the castle are home to an abundance of wild plants and animals, many of which you can see on the nature trail. Wild visitors to the woods include roe deer, which during the winter months can often be spotted sheltering among the trees, and the natterjack toad, whose only breeding colonies in Scotland are around the Solway Firth.

Meadowsweet, identifiable by its white, fernlike foliage, is one of several important plants growing at Caerlaverock. Before the advent of carpets, people laid down meadowsweet on floors, where the crushed stalks emitted the sweet smell from which the plant derives its name. More recently, scientists have produced salicylic acid from meadowsweet buds to form the basis of aspirin (which takes its name from the botanical term for the plant, *spiraea*).

Above top: While it is impossible to age coppiced trees such as this willow, many trees at Caerlaverock are hundreds of years old, their lives prolonged by the very act of coppicing.

Above: Delicate meadowsweet was once used as a sweet-smelling floor covering.

Below: A young roe deer. The woods around Caerlaverock provide deer and other animals with food and shelter.

THE OLD CASTLE

In the late 1990s archaeologists excavating the old castle found that its outer defences dated from about 950. This discovery confirms that the Maxwells' construction of around 1220 was in fact the re-defending of an old fort built for the lords of Nithsdale.

When built, the castle lay close to the Solway shore (now some 800m away), and remains of a dried-up harbour are visible in the trees to the south. The approach to the castle was through an outer defended enclosure, or bailey, which occupied five or six times as much land as the castle and contained domestic and estate buildings that supported the Maxwell household. (You can see traces of the bailey's banks and ditches as you walk back through the woods to the visitor centre.)

THE OLD CASTLE INTERIOR

The castle itself was defended by a timber palisade which enclosed a timber hall and stone chamber-block. By 1250, a stone curtain wall had replaced the palisade, and the wood-built hall similarly gave way to stone. Square towers were subsequently added to three of the four corners of the curtain wall. These towers would have been two storeys high and provided accommodation as well as better defence. Archaeologists have laid out the surviving foundations of these stone structures, and indicated the missing parts with modern materials.

The cobbled path leads from the entrance across the courtyard to a forestair. This gave access to the first floor of the chamber-block, which housed the Maxwell family on two floors. The stone pads on the ground supported an external covered walkway with a lean-to roof giving sheltered access between the chamber-block and the great hall. This hall, entered directly from the courtyard, was the chief public space in the castle, where justice was dispensed and estate business transacted. It was also a place of feasting and entertainment, with Lord and Lady Maxwell occupying pride of place at the high table in the east end. From here the family had direct access not only to their private chambers but also to a latrine block. A stone drain running along the outside of the great hall collected water from the eaves as well as the courtyard and channelled it away through the curtain wall into the moat.

Above: The site of the old castle, which was previously occupied by a 10th-century fort.

Opposite: An artist's impression of how the old castle and harbour might have appeared around 1260, shortly before the Maxwells relocated to the new castle.

Below: These 13th-century glass fragments, found during excavations of the old castle's great hall floor, are the only pieces of glass with Arabic lettering ever discovered from a Scottish site. They were once part of a vessel which may have been brought to Caerlaverock from Syria as a souvenir of the Crusades.

THE STORY OF
CAERLAVEROCK
CASTLE

T hanks to its strategic position on the Solway Firth, Caerlaverock was a border-control point long before the Wars of Independence between Scotland and England. An Iron-Age fort once crowned the summit of Ward Law, the hill overlooking the castle from the north. This defence gave way to another fort, built by the Romans. Tacitus, the biographer of Agricola, the Roman governor of Britain, wrote of a sea-borne invasion across the Solway in AD 82. It is possible that the legionaries landed on Caerlaverock's shore.

FROM ROMANS TO MAXWELLS

When the Romans finally abandoned southern Scotland in the 4th century, into the vacuum stepped the Britons of Strathclyde. It now seems likely that the British lords of Strath Nith operated from what became the old castle site. Around 1157, Lord Radulph, son of Dunegal, granted land at 'Karlaueroc' to Holm Cultram Abbey, which lay directly across the Solway in Cumberland and was founded by David I of Scotland a short time earlier (Cumbria being then part of the kingdom of Scotland). The monks may have established a grange, or estate farm, at Caerlaverock, from where they could ship produce to the abbey via its harbour at Skinburness, near Silloth.

By the mid-12th century, however, the political landscape was once again changing. Following David I's death at Carlisle in 1153, Scotland's hold over Cumbria weakened, and within 20 years it had gone. Caerlaverock became a Border post again, at a time when the kings of Scots needed trusted men to defend the realm. Around 1220, therefore, Alexander II granted the barony of Caerlaverock to his chamberlain, Sir John de Maccuswell (Maxwell). The Maxwells, incomers from the eastern Borders, were a noble family, holding the prestigious office of sheriff of Teviotdale. The estate soon became the family's principal seat.

Opposite: A 19th-century illustration of Caerlaverock's gatehouse and flanking towers. The medieval drawbridge had long since collapsed into the moat; the modern bridge was constructed in the 1960s.

TIMELINE

AD 82

ROMAN ADVANCE
Roman legionaries cross the Solway Firth and land near Caerlaverock. They build a fort on the summit of Ward Law (right).

c.1220

ROYAL GRANT
Alexander II grants Caerlaverock to his loyal chamberlain, Sir John de Maccuswell (Maxwell).

A TALE OF TWO CASTLES

Sir John de Maxwell built his castle beside the Caerlaverock Burn at the point where it runs into the Solway Firth. The family spent 50 years there, sufficient time for them to convert their original timber manor house into an impressive stone residence. But after two generations they had outgrown the small site. When Sir Herbert, John's nephew, became lord of Caerlaverock around 1266, he decided to relocate to a new site 200m away, where he could build a much grander residence. The fact that the site of the old castle was prone to flooding probably contributed to the decision.

The building of the new castle was under way by 1277, since records show that in the spring of that year the timbers for the drawbridge were felled. Its construction represented an enormous investment in time and money by Sir Herbert. It was not unlike that built for the earl of Mar at Kildrummy, except for its smaller size and uniquely triangular shape. Sir Herbert's castle lay at the heart of a much larger outer enclosure, stretching from the harbour to the south (constructed for the old castle but retained) to the present-day visitor centre. This space accommodated the 'castletoun', where the stables, workshops, brewhouses and bakehouses were situated.

In 1291 Sir Herbert was one of the nobles appointed to choose a successor to Margaret, the daughter of Alexander III who died aged only seven years. But when Edward I invaded Scotland in 1296, ending King John's reign, the peace enjoyed by the Maxwells ended too. Caerlaverock Castle, situated on the Anglo-Scottish Border, was inevitably caught up in the ensuing power struggle.

Above: Kildrummy Castle, like Caerlaverock, was a state-of-the-art construction in the 13th century. Both castles demonstrated their owners' awareness of international developments in castle building.

Opposite: The old and new castles at Caerlaverock, with the mudflats of the Solway Firth beyond. In the Middle Ages the coastline lay just a short distance from the old castle, which was therefore liable to flooding.

1250   1277

FROM THE OLD...
Sir John de Maccuswell completes building the old castle.

...TO THE NEW
Sir Herbert de Maxwell, the nephew of Sir John, relocates to the new castle.

THE SIEGE OF 1300

In the aftermath of the English invasion, many Scots swore loyalty to Edward I; among them were Herbert Maxwell of Caerlaverock and his son, John. But the Scots soon began to resist their new English overlord. Undaunted, Edward returned time and again, and in 1300 invaded Galloway, one of the strongest centres of resistance. Caerlaverock Castle was a prime target for his wrath.

Although it was a marginal incident in the turbulent events of the time, the siege of Caerlaverock in 1300 has become one of the best known military operations of the Wars, thanks to a detailed account of it written by a herald in Edward's army. The poem, accompanied by a colourful account of the heraldry flaunted by the English knights, is redolent of chivalry and martial prowess. 'Caerlaverock', it tells us, 'was so strong a castle that it feared no siege before the King came there, for it would never have had to surrender, provided that it was well supplied, when the need arose, with men, engines and provisions.'

The odds were overwhelmingly in the English army's favour. Edward brought 87 knights and 3,000 men to Caerlaverock, while the castle's defence fell to Robert de Cunningham, valet to the Steward of Scotland, with a garrison of just 60 men. Neither Herbert nor John Maxwell was in the castle at the time. The English force pitched their brightly coloured camp, the insides of their tents strewn with herbs and flowers. Then their siege engines arrived, brought from the castles of Lochmaben, Carlisle, Roxburgh, Jedburgh and Skinburness.

1296   1300

WARS OF INDEPENDENCE
Edward I of England invades Scotland to start the Wars of Independence.

CAERLAVEROCK CAPTURED
Edward besieges and captures the castle in under two days.

As the poet observed: '[the castle] will not be taken by check with a rook, but there will be projectiles thrown and engines raised and poised'. Within two days, de Cunningham's garrison surrendered. The poem tells of the English beholding 'with much astonishment' the tiny force which had opposed them. Some were hanged from the castle walls, while the rest were allowed to walk free.

Below: Edward I's siege of Caerlaverock, depicted in this artist's impression, saw the might of the English army brought to bear on a Scots garrison of 60 soldiers.

THE CASTLE AND THE WARS WITH ENGLAND

The castle remained in English hands until 1312, when the keeper was none other than Sir Eustace Maxwell, who demonstrated the family's ability to 'bend with the wind'. Shortly afterwards, he changed sides and declared for King Robert I (the Bruce). He was besieged in his castle, but held out, only to be ordered by Robert to demolish the castle. A functioning castle was a potential bolt-hole for the English.

The accession of Robert's son David II in 1329, and the reopening of hostilities between Scotland and England, was the signal for Sir Eustace to change allegiance once more. The traditional loyalties of the Maxwells were to the Balliols and not to the Bruces, and when Edward Balliol (the son of King John) was crowned king at Scone in 1332, Sir Eustace repaired and garrisoned Caerlaverock, placing it at Balliol's disposal.

Opposite: This replica trebuchet serves as a reminder of the attacks Caerlaverock faced in the 14th century. A trebuchet worked a little bit like a seesaw – the long arm was winched down, fitted with a missile and then released, the weight on the short arm providing the counterpoise.

Below: The memorial to Edward I looms over the place where he died in 1307, Burgh-by-Sands, on the English side of the Solway Estuary. Edward was about to invade Scotland yet again.

The repair of the drawbridge in the 1330s has been confirmed by archaeologists tree-ring dating the bridge timbers in the moat. The story thereafter is obscure until about 1356, when Roger Kirkpatrick, the sheriff of Dumfries, is recorded as having returned the whole of Nithsdale to the Scottish Crown. Kirkpatrick captured the castles of Dalswinton and Caerlaverock by 'force and valour and demolished them to the ground'.

Below: An assortment of stone trebuchet balls and iron cannon balls, discovered in the grounds of Caerlaverock Castle. Cannons were used in siege warfare from the 15th century.

1312

SIDING WITH ENGLAND
Sir Eustace Maxwell holds the castle for England against Robert I but soon switches sides. He demolishes the castle.

1332

SWITCHING AGAIN
Sir Eustace Maxwell changes sides once again, and refortifies the castle. These excavated drawbridge timbers date to this time.

WAR AND PEACE

Despite their pro-Balliol stance during the Wars of Independence, the Maxwells held on to Caerlaverock. Rebuilding work began in the 1370s, and much of what stands today dates from this time. The process was a lengthy affair and seems only to have been completed in the later 15th century. By then, Herbert Maxwell had been created Lord Maxwell, and Robert, the second lord, warden of the Scottish West March. By the time the builders had finished, the gatehouse defences had been strengthened and the domestic accommodation greatly improved. The splendid machicolations crowning the castle walls and the finely carved details in the west range probably date to Robert's time.

A RISING POWER

In 1513, the Maxwells were left bereft following the disaster at Flodden, losing John, fourth lord, and three of his brothers in that bloody battle against the English army of Henry VIII. But the family recovered well, and in 1536 Robert, fifth lord, became

Above: An English spy's distorted perspective of Caerlaverock Castle, drawn between 1563 and 1566, suggests what the portcullis and drawbridge may then have looked like.

regent of Scotland during James V's temporary absence in France. By now the family controlled most of the major places of strength in the area, including the mighty castles of Lochmaben and Threave, as well as Caerlaverock.

Caerlaverock Castle again figured in the conflicts between Scotland and England that bedevilled the 16th century. In 1542, James V visited the castle before the battle of Solway Moss, which resulted not only in defeat for the Scots but in the capture of Robert, fifth Lord Maxwell. Released shortly after, he was again captured in May 1544, leaving the castle to fall to the English (although the Scots retook it the following year). In 1570 an English army, this time led by the earl of Sussex, once more besieged and took Caerlaverock. Although it is said that Sussex 'threw down' the castle, there is little evidence in the present structure for this demolition.

NEW DEFENCES

Throughout all this time, the Maxwells remained devout Catholics. Even after the Reformation of 1560, they played a dangerous game, which included a trip to Spain in the 1580s to help arrange the Armada invasion. Possibly because of his pro-Spanish, Catholic stance, in 1593, Robert, eighth lord, was said to be making 'great fortifications and [had] many men working at his house'. Excavations in front of the castle in the 1960s revealed that the outer moat dates from around this time. The moat was crossed by a bridge on a different alignment from the one traversing the inner moat, thus creating a more awkward 'dog-legged' approach. Still visible beyond this outer bridge is a high grassy bank that may well be the remains of a ravelin (a triangular artillery defence) protecting this new route into the castle. A later account refers to 'casements [gun emplacements] upon the rampart with a parapet fenced with a palisade'.

Above: Fortifications grafted onto the castle included the 15th-century machicolations (top), through which defenders hurled missiles, and the 16th-century gun holes, added to the gatehouse's flanking towers to accommodate mounted guns.

1542

1593

ROYAL VISIT
King James V visits the castle shortly before his defeat at the battle of Solway Moss.

REFORTIFICATION
Robert, eighth lord Maxwell, greatly strengthens his castle.

THE UNION OF THE CROWNS

In 1603, James VI's accession to the English throne as James I brought peace to the Border country for the first time in centuries. The tranquillity led to a new-found confidence amongst the marcher lords. By 1634, Robert Maxwell, created earl of Nithsdale in 1620, was overseeing yet more building works within Caerlaverock's walls. The result, his Nithsdale Lodging, was an elegant Renaissance mansion, described by one contemporary as 'that dainty fabrick'.

By 1640, however, any sense of peace was shattered. Charles I had inherited none of his father's skill as a politician but all of his problems. The earl of Nithsdale was one of his most loyal supporters, but Charles warned him to look to himself when the truce with his Scottish subjects broke down in that year in the face of the attempt to impose Episcopalianism in Scotland. The earl bravely resisted the Covenanting army led by Lieutenant-Colonel John Home, garrisoning his castle with 200 soldiers. They gallantly held out for 13 weeks before the hopelessness of his position forced the earl to surrender.

THE TRAPPINGS OF WEALTH

An inventory taken at the time gives a fascinating picture of the furniture and furnishings then in the castle. They included: five beds, two of silk and three of cloth, each with silk fringes and a silk counterpane tester decorated with braid and silk lace; accompanying stools and chairs to match; feather beds (mattresses), blankets, bolsters and pillows to serve the timber beds; 10 lesser beds, 20 servants' beds and 40 carpets; a library of books; and trunks full of sheets, pillowcases, table cloths, napkins and towels. These are the furnishings of a comfortable country house, not a medieval fortress.

Above: This female stone column, known as a caryatid, once formed one side of an elaborate fireplace in the Nithsdale Lodging.

Opposite: A 19th-century etching of the castle courtyard by R.W. Billings. The Nithsdale Lodging, on the right-hand side, represented the last phase of building within the castle.

1620	1634

FROM LORD TO EARL
Robert Maxwell is created earl of Nithsdale.

RENAISSANCE SPLENDOUR
Earl Robert builds the Nithsdale Lodging – 'that dainty fabrick'.

1640   1776

LAST STAND
Earl Robert surrenders
to the Covenanters after
a 13-week siege.

OLD GRAFFITI
Richard Blennerhasset
leaves his mark on the
gatehouse hall.

THE TWILIGHT OF THE CASTLE

After the 1640 siege the castle was partially dismantled by the Covenanters to render it incapable of further defence. (The Covenanters did much the same to the earl's castle at Threave, which they captured in the same campaign.) This time there was no reprieve for the Maxwell family. Redundant both as fortress and as residence, Caerlaverock rapidly fell into decay, becoming a romantic retreat for visitors who wished to paint it, write about it or simply to marvel at the past which its ivy-clad walls evoked. One such visitor was Richard Blennerhasset, a Catholic, in 1776. He left his mark on the south wall of the hall in the gatehouse. His initials can also be seen in Carlisle Cathedral, where he sheltered for a time.

Caerlaverock Castle passed by inheritance through the family of Herries, a branch of the Maxwells, to the dukes of Norfolk. In 1946, the 16th duke placed it in state care. Since then it has lost its romantic ivy but gained a secure future so that visitors might enjoy, and learn from, its remains.

1946

STATE CARE
The 16th Duke of Norfolk entrusts the castle into state care.

Main image opposite:
A 19th-century illustration of the castle from the south. Most of the south curtain wall was demolished after the final siege of the castle in 1640.

Above: In the Victorian period, Caerlaverock Castle's ivy-covered walls attracted artists like R.P. Leitch, whose watercolour depicts a romantic Scottish ruin.

Caerlaverock Castle is one of over 30 Historic Scotland sites in Dumfries and Galloway, a selection of which is shown below.

New Abbey Corn Mill

↗ 7m S of Dumfries on the A710

🕐 Open all year **Winter:** closed Thu/Fri

📞 01387 850260

🚗 Approx 12 miles from Caerlaverock Castle

Facilities
🛈 ♿ ⊞

Sweetheart Abbey

↗ In New Abbey village on the A710

🕐 Open all year **Winter:** closed Thu/Fri

📞 01387 850397

🚗 Approx 12 miles from Caerlaverock Castle

Facilities
🅿 🚌 🚻 ♿ ⊞

MacLellan's Castle

↗ In Kirkcudbright on the A711

🕐 Open summer only

📞 01557 331856

🚗 Approx 33 miles from Caerlaverock Castle

Facilities
🚻 ♿ ⊞

Threave Castle

↗ 3m W of Castle Douglas on the A75

🕐 Open summer only

📞 07711 223101

🚗 Approx 17 miles from Caerlaverock Castle

Facilities
🅿 🚌 🚻 ♿ ⛱ ⊞

For more information on all Historic Scotland sites, visit **www.historic-scotland.gov.uk**
To order a wide range of products and tickets, visit **www.historic-scotland.gov.uk/shop**

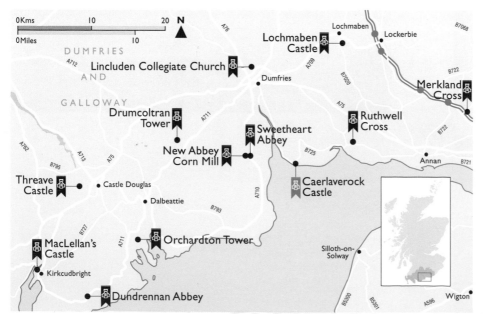

Key to facilities

Admission charge	⊞
Bus/coach parking	🚌
Car parking	🅿
Interpretive display	🛈
Picnic area	⛱
Reasonable wheelchair access	♿
Shop	🛍
Toilets	🚻
Visitor centre	🛈

NB: Strong footwear is recommended for visitors to Threave Castle.